ROWDEAN
KURASCH-MACHARZINA

"Beyond the Dollar: Transforming Your Mindest for Lifelong Financial Success"

Copyright © 2024 by Rowdean Kurasch-Macharzina

All rights reserved. No part of this publication may be reproduced, stored or transmitted in any form or by any means, electronic, mechanical, photocopying, recording, scanning, or otherwise without written permission from the publisher. It is illegal to copy this book, post it to a website, or distribute it by any other means without permission.

Rowdean Kurasch-Macharzina asserts the moral right to be identified as the author of this work.

Rowdean Kurasch-Macharzina has no responsibility for the persistence or accuracy of URLs for external or third-party Internet Websites referred to in this publication and does not guarantee that any content on such Websites is, or will remain, accurate or appropriate.

Designations used by companies to distinguish their products are often claimed as trademarks. All brand names and product names used in this book and on its cover are trade names, service marks, trademarks and registered trademarks of their respective owners. The publishers and the book are not associated with any product or vendor mentioned in this book. None of the companies referenced within the book have endorsed the book.

First edition

This book was professionally typeset on Reedsy.
Find out more at reedsy.com

"Your economic security does not lie in your job; it lies in your own power to produce—to think, to learn, to create, to adapt." — Stephen Covey

Contents

Introduction		1
1	The Foundation of Wealth: Mindset Matters	3
2	Reprogramming Your Mind for Success	8
3	The Psychology of Money	14
4	Setting Clear Financial Goals	20
5	Building Wealth-Building Habits	27
6	Smart Investing: Protecting and Growing Your Wealth	34
7	Managing and Growing Your Wealth	41
8	Financial Independence: Achieving Freedom and Early...	48
9	leaving a Legacy: Ensuring Your Wealth and Wisdom Live On	56
10	Celebrating Your Journey and Paying It Forward	63
11	Conclusion	70
About the Author		73

Introduction

Beyond the Dollar: Transforming Your Mindset for Lifelong Financial Success

In a world where wealth is often measured solely by the numbers in our bank accounts, it's easy to lose sight of what true financial success really means. We chase after the next promotion, the next investment opportunity, the next big purchase, all in the hope that these will bring us the security and happiness we crave. But what if the key to lifelong financial success isn't just about accumulating more money? What if the real secret lies in transforming the way we think about wealth, success, and ultimately, life itself?

"Beyond the Dollar" invites you to embark on a journey that goes deeper than the pursuit of material wealth. This book is not just about learning how to manage your finances—it's about redefining your relationship with money, cultivating a mindset that aligns with your values, and achieving a sense of fulfillment that goes beyond the balance sheet.

Throughout these pages, we'll explore the power of mindset and how it influences every aspect of your financial life.

"BEYOND THE DOLLAR: TRANSFORMING YOUR MINDEST FOR LIFELONG FINANCIAL SUCCESS"

You'll discover practical strategies for building wealth, but more importantly, you'll learn how to sustain that wealth by embracing a holistic approach to success. We'll delve into the psychology of money, the importance of aligning your financial goals with your personal values, and the ways in which true wealth extends far beyond mere dollars and cents.

Whether you're just starting out on your financial journey or you're looking to take your wealth-building efforts to the next level, this book will provide you with the tools and insights you need to transform your mindset and achieve lasting financial success. By the end, you'll understand that true financial freedom isn't just about having more—it's about being more, doing more, and living a life that is rich in every sense of the word.

So, are you ready to go beyond the dollar and unlock the secrets to lifelong financial success? Let's get started. Your journey to a richer, more fulfilling life begins here.

1

The Foundation of Wealth: Mindset Matters

"BEYOND THE DOLLAR: TRANSFORMING YOUR MINDEST FOR LIFELONG FINANCIAL SUCCESS"

Understanding The Power of The Mindset

Imagine a house built on shaky ground—it doesn't matter how beautiful the exterior is, or how grand the rooms are, because eventually, that house will crumble. The same can be said for wealth. You might have the best financial strategies or the smartest investment plans, but if your mindset isn't solid, everything can come crashing down.

Your mindset is the foundation upon which your financial success is built. It's the lens through which you view money, wealth, and your own potential. If you believe that you're destined to struggle financially, that belief will guide your actions, often leading to poor decisions and missed opportunities. On the other hand, if you believe that you have the ability to grow and learn, that mindset will push you toward better decisions and, ultimately, greater financial success.

The Fixed vs. Growth Mindset

To really understand how mindset impacts wealth, let's dive into two powerful concepts: the fixed mindset and the growth mindset.

The Fixed Mindset:
People with a fixed mindset believe that their abilities, intelligence, and talents are set in stone. They think they're either "good" or "bad" with money, and there's nothing they can do to change that. This kind of thinking can be a major roadblock on the path to wealth. If you believe you're inherently bad at managing money, you're less likely to take the steps necessary to improve. You might avoid learning about finances, skip opportunities to invest, or simply give up at the first sign of a challenge.

The Growth Mindset:
In contrast, people with a growth mindset believe that they can develop their abilities through hard work, learning, and persistence. When it comes to finances, this mindset is a game-changer. With a growth mindset, you understand that while

you might not know everything about money right now, you can learn and improve. You're willing to take on challenges, seek out new information, and keep pushing forward, even when things get tough.

Think of the growth mindset as the fertile soil where the seeds of your financial future can truly flourish. With this mindset, the sky's the limit.

How Your Beliefs Shape Your Financial Reality

Now that we've covered the basics of mindset, let's explore how your beliefs—often formed in childhood—shape your financial reality.

Beliefs and Money:
From a young age, we absorb beliefs about money from our families, society, and personal experiences. If you grew up hearing phrases like "money doesn't grow on trees" or "we can't afford that," you might have internalized the idea that money is scarce or hard to come by. These beliefs stick with us and influence how we think about and handle money as adults.

For example, if you believe that rich people are greedy or that money is evil, you might subconsciously sabotage your own financial success. You might avoid pursuing opportunities that could make you wealthy or feel guilty about earning more money. On the flip side, if you believe that money is a tool for freedom and that there's plenty to go around, you'll likely be more open to financial opportunities and feel confident in your ability to create wealth.

Changing the Narrative:
The good news is, you have the power to change your beliefs. It starts with awareness—recognizing the beliefs you hold about money—and then consciously choosing to adopt new, more empowering beliefs. Instead of telling yourself, "I'm not good with money," start saying, "I'm learning to manage my money wisely." This simple shift can have a profound impact on your financial reality.

As you move forward in this book, you'll learn more about how to transform your mindset and beliefs, setting the stage for lifelong financial success. Remember, wealth isn't just about the numbers in your bank account; it's about the thoughts in your mind.

In Summary:
This chapter has laid the groundwork for your wealth-building journey. Your mindset is the foundation upon which everything else is built. By embracing a growth mindset and actively working to change limiting beliefs, you're setting yourself up for success. As we move into the next chapter, you'll learn how to reprogram your mind for even greater financial success.

Your journey to wealth starts now—with the right mindset, there's nothing you can't achieve.

2

Reprogramming Your Mind for Success

Identifying Limiting Beliefs

Before you can reach the next level in your financial journey, it's crucial to identify what might be holding you back. Often, the biggest obstacles aren't external—they're internal. These obstacles are known as limiting beliefs, and they're like invisible chains that keep you stuck in place.

What Are Limiting Beliefs?

Limiting beliefs are deeply ingrained thoughts or assumptions that limit your potential. They're the little voices in your head that say, "I'll never be rich," "I'm just not good with money," or "Success is for other people, not me." These beliefs often stem from past experiences, cultural influences, or things you've heard growing up. They can be sneaky, operating under the surface and influencing your decisions without you even realizing it.

Common Limiting Beliefs:

Here are a few examples of limiting beliefs that many people hold:
"Money is the root of all evil."
If you believe this, you might subconsciously push wealth away,
fearing it will corrupt you.

"I'm not smart enough to be rich."
This belief can prevent you from even trying to learn about finances
or pursuing wealth-building opportunities.

"Rich people are greedy."
Holding onto this belief might cause you to feel guilty
or ashamed about wanting to build wealth.

Self-Assessment:
Take a moment to reflect on your own beliefs about money. Ask yourself:

- What did I hear about money growing up?
- How do I feel when I think about becoming wealthy?
- Do I believe I deserve to be financially successful?

Write down any limiting beliefs you identify. The simple act of

recognizing
  these beliefs is the first step in overcoming them.

Tools and Techniques to Shift Your Money Mindset

Now that you've identified your limiting beliefs, it's time to do something about them. Just like you'd train your body to get stronger, you can train your mind to think differently about money. Here are some powerful tools and techniques to help you shift your mindset.

Mindset Shifting Techniques:
  Journaling: Start a money journal where you write down your thoughts,
  feelings, and beliefs about money.
  This practice can help you uncover deep-seated beliefs and track your progress
  as you work to change them.
  Positive Affirmations: are positive statements that you repeat to yourself
  to help rewire your brain.
  For example, if you've been telling yourself, "I'll never be rich,"
  try replacing that with, "I am capable of building wealth."
  Visualization: Spend a few minutes each day visualizing yourself living a wealthy life. Imagine what it would feel like to have financial freedom.
  Picture the details—your dream home, the freedom to travel, the peace of mind that comes with financial security.

Rephrasing Negative Thoughts:
When you catch yourself thinking a negative thought about money, challenge it.

For example, if you think, "**I can't afford tha**t," rephrase it as, "**How can I afford that?**"

This subtle shift opens your mind to possibilities instead of shutting them down.

By consistently rephrasing your thoughts, you'll start to see money in a more positive and empowering light.

The Role of Affirmations and Visualization

Let's dive deeper into two of the most effective tools for reprogramming your mind: affirmations and visualization.

Affirmations for Wealth:
Affirmations work by repeatedly exposing your mind to positive, empowering statements, gradually replacing the old, limiting beliefs. The key to making affirmations effective is to say them with conviction and consistency. Here are a few powerful money-related affirmations you can use:

- "I am worthy of financial success."
- "Money flows to me easily and effortlessly."
- "I am open to new opportunities to create wealth."
- "Every day, I am getting better at managing my money."

Say these affirmations out loud every morning, or write them down in your journal.

The more you repeat them, the more they'll start to shape your reality.

Visualization Exercises:

Visualization is like mental rehearsal for success.

When you visualize your goals, your brain doesn't fully distinguish between

the imagined experience and real-life experiences, which makes visualization

a powerful tool for creating the life you want.

Here's a simple visualization exercise to try:

- **Find a quiet place where you won't be disturbed.**
- **Close your eyes and take a few deep breaths to relax.**
- **Picture yourself in the future, living your ideal wealthy life.**
- **What do you see?**
- **Where are you? What are you doing? How do you feel?**
- **Engage all your senses in the visualization.**
- **Imagine the sounds, smells, and feelings associated with your wealthy life.**
- **Spend a few minutes fully immersing yourself in this vision.**
- **The more vividly you can imagine it, the more powerful the exercise will be.**

Practice this visualization regularly, and watch as your mindset—and your life—begins to shift in alignment with your goals.

In Summary:

In this chapter, you've taken the crucial steps to reprogram your mind for financial success. By identifying and challenging your limiting beliefs, adopting positive affirmations, and regularly visualizing your goals, you're actively reshaping your financial reality. Remember, your mind is your most powerful asset on the road to wealth—use it wisely, and there's no limit to what you can achieve.

Next, we'll explore the fascinating psychology of money and how your emotions and past experiences play a significant role in your financial decisions. The journey continues, and with each chapter, you're getting closer to transforming your financial life beyond the dollar.

3

The Psychology of Money

The Emotional Relationship with Money

Money isn't just numbers in a bank account or bills in your wallet—it's deeply emotional. For many of us, the thought of money can bring up a whole range of feelings, from joy and excitement to fear and anxiety. Understanding this emotional connection is key to mastering your finances.

Money as an Emotional Trigger:
Think about the last time you made a financial decision. Whether it was buying something expensive, paying off a debt, or even just checking your bank balance, chances are it stirred up some feelings. Maybe you felt a rush of excitement when you bought something you've wanted for a while, or perhaps you felt a pit in your stomach when looking at your credit card bill. These emotions are normal, but they can sometimes lead us astray.

For example, if you're feeling stressed or insecure, you might find yourself overspending on things you don't need as a way to cope. Or, if you're overly cautious, you might hoard money and miss out on opportunities to invest or enjoy life. The first step to taking control of your financial life is recognizing these emotional triggers and understanding how they influence your behavior.

Understanding Emotional Triggers:
Take a moment to reflect on your recent financial decisions. Ask yourself:

- **What emotions were driving my decision?**

- Was I feeling confident, anxious, impulsive, or guilty?
- How did these emotions affect the outcome?

By becoming more aware of your emotional responses to money, you can start making more thoughtful and rational financial choices.

How Past Experiences Influence Your Financial Decisions

We all carry the weight of our past experiences, and these can have a powerful impact on how we handle money today. The way you grew up, the lessons you learned from your parents, and even your past financial successes or failures all shape your current financial habits.

The Impact of Past Experiences:
 Let's say you grew up in a household where money was tight, and your parents often argued about it. This experience might lead you to associate money with stress and conflict, which could cause you to avoid dealing with your finances or feel anxious about spending money, even when you have enough.

On the other hand, if you were raised in a family where money was plentiful but spending was careless, you might struggle with managing your money as an adult, spending freely without thinking about the consequences.

These past experiences create a mental framework that influences your financial decisions, often without you even realizing it.

Healing Financial Wounds:
The good news is that you can heal from these past experiences and develop a healthier relationship with money. Here's how:

- **Acknowledge the Past**: Reflect on your financial upbringing and identify any patterns or attitudes that might be holding you back. Were you taught that money is scarce? Did you learn to equate wealth with happiness? Acknowledging these patterns is the first step to breaking free from them.

-**Forgive Yourself and Others:**If you've made financial mistakes in the past, it's important to forgive yourself. Likewise, if your parents or others influenced your negative attitudes toward money, practice forgiveness toward them too. This will help you let go of any lingering guilt or resentment that's affecting your financial decisions.

- **Create New Financial Stories**: Replace those old, limiting beliefs with new, empowering ones. For example, instead of saying, "I'm bad with money," start saying, "I'm learning to manage my finances effectively." These new stories will help you build a healthier, more positive relationship with money.

Developing a Healthy Attitude Toward Wealth

Now that you understand the emotional and psychological factors that influence your relationship with money, it's time to cultivate a healthier, more positive attitude toward wealth. This new attitude will be the key to achieving financial success and happiness.

Redefining Wealth:

Wealth isn't just about having a lot of money. It's about living a life of abundance, security, and freedom. Take a moment to redefine what wealth means to you personally. Is it the freedom to travel? The ability to take care of your family? The peace of mind that comes with knowing you're financially secure? By focusing on what wealth truly means to you, you'll be more motivated to achieve it.

Embracing Abundance:

One of the most powerful shifts you can make in your mindset is moving from a scarcity mentality to an abundance mentality. A scarcity mentality is the belief that there's never enough—that money is limited, and you have to fight to get your share. This mindset can lead to fear, anxiety, and even greed.

In contrast, an abundance mentality is the belief that there's plenty of wealth to go around, and that you can create more for yourself and others. This mindset encourages generosity, optimism, and confidence in your financial decisions. Embracing abundance means trusting that you have the ability to create wealth and that doing so doesn't take away from others—instead, it adds to the overall wealth in the world.

In Summary:

This chapter has taken you on a journey through the emotional and psychological landscape of money. By understanding your emotional relationship with money, reflecting on your past experiences, and developing a healthier attitude toward wealth, you're laying the groundwork for a more prosperous and fulfilling financial life.

As we move forward, we'll dive into setting clear financial goals and creating a road map for achieving the wealth you desire. Remember, money is not just a tool—it's a reflection of your mindset and emotions. Master these, and you're well on your way to mastering your financial future.

4

Setting Clear Financial Goals

The Power of Purposeful Goals

Imagine setting out on a road trip without a destination. You'd waste time, gas, and energy driving around aimlessly. The same goes for your financial journey. Without clear, purposeful goals, you might find yourself drifting, unsure of where you're going or how to get there. Setting financial goals is like plugging your destination into a GPS—it guides your actions and helps you stay on track.

Why Goals Matter:

Goals give your financial life direction and purpose. They turn vague desires, like "I want to be rich," into specific, actionable steps. For example, "I want to save $10,000 in the next year" is a concrete goal that you can plan for and track. Goals also keep you motivated. When you see progress, even small wins, it builds momentum and encourages you to keep going.

The Ripple Effect:

Financial goals don't just impact your bank account—they influence every area of your life. Achieving financial security can reduce stress, give you more freedom, and improve your relationships. It's not just about money; it's about creating the life you want.

SMART Goals: Your Blueprint for Success

To set yourself up for success, your goals should be SMART:

Specific, Measurable, Achievable, Relevant, and Time-bound. This framework turns your financial dreams into practical steps you can actually follow.

1. **Specific**:

Your goals should be clear and specific. Instead of saying, "I want to save more money," specify exactly what you want to achieve. For example, "I want to save $5,000 for a down payment on a car." The more specific your goal, the easier it is to create a plan to reach it.

2.**Measurable**:

You need to track your progress to stay motivated.

A measurable goal might be, "I will save $500 each month until I reach $5,000."

This way, you can measure your progress and know exactly when you've achieved your goal.

3. **Achievable**:

While it's important to challenge yourself, your goals should still be realistic.

If you set a goal that's too far out of reach, you might get discouraged and give up.

Ask yourself, "Is this goal achievable with my current income and expenses?"

If the answer is no, adjust your goal to make it more attainable.

4. **Relevant**:

Your financial goals should align with your overall life goals. Ask yourself, "Why is this goal important to me?" If your goal is to save for a home, think about how home ownership fits into your bigger picture—maybe it's about stability, creating a family space, or investing in your future.

5. Time-bound:

Every goal needs a deadline. A time-bound goal might be, "I will save $5,000 by December 31st.Deadlines create a sense of urgency and help you stay focused.

Without a time frame, it's easy to procrastinate and let your goals slip away.

Short-Term vs. Long-Term Goals

When setting financial goals, it's important to distinguish between short-term and long-term goals. Both are essential, but they serve different purposes.

Short Term Goals:

These are goals you can achieve within a few months to a couple of years. They're the immediate steps that lead to bigger financial milestones. Examples of short-term goals include:

- **Building an emergency fund**
- **Paying off credit card debt**
- **Saving for a vacation or a big purchase**

Long-Term Goals:

These are goals that require years of planning and saving.

They often involve larger sums of money and have a more significant impact on your financial future.

Examples of long-term goals include:

- **Saving for retirement**
- **Paying off your mortgage**
- **Funding your children's education**

Balancing Both:

It's important to balance short-term and long-term goals. Focusing too much on the short term can leave you unprepared for the future, while only thinking long-term can make it hard to stay motivated. Create a mix of both to ensure you're making progress now and securing your future.

Creating a Financial Road map

Now that you've identified your goals, it's time to create a road map to achieve them. This road map is your action plan—step-by-step instructions on how to reach each of your goals.

1. **Prioritize Your Goals**:

Start by listing all your financial goals, both short-term and long-term. Then, prioritize them based on their importance and urgency. For example, building an emergency fund might take priority over saving for a new car.

2. **Break It Down:**

For each goal, break it down into smaller, manageable steps. For example, if your goal is to save $10,000 in a year, you might break that down into saving $833 each month or $192 each week. Smaller steps make big goals feel less overwhelming.

3. **Set Milestones**:
Milestones are like checkpoints along your journey. They help you stay on track and celebrate your progress. For example, if your goal is to pay off $5,000 in debt, a milestone might be paying off the first $1,000.

4. **Adjust as Needed**:
Life is unpredictable, and your goals might need to change along the way. Don't be afraid to adjust your road map as needed. If you get a raise, you might be able to save more each month. If unexpected expenses come up, you might need to extend your timeline. Flexibility is key to staying on track.

In Summary:

In this chapter, you've learned the importance of setting clear, purposeful financial goals and how to use the SMART framework to turn your dreams into actionable plans. By balancing short-term and long-term goals and creating a detailed road map, you're setting yourself up for success. Remember, goals aren't just about reaching a destination—they're about creating a journey that leads to lasting financial success and a fulfilling life.

Next, we'll dive into the habits and behaviors that support your goals and help you stay on track. With your goals in place, the next step is to build the daily routines that will bring you closer to financial freedom.

5

Building Wealth-Building Habits

The Power of Habits

Habits are the invisible force that shapes your life, including your financial future. While big decisions and life-changing events can impact your finances, it's the small, everyday habits that have the most lasting effect. Just like daily exercise can transform your health over time, consistent financial habits can lead to significant wealth accumulation. The key to financial success isn't about making one big leap—it's about making small, steady steps every day.

The Daily Habits of Financially Successful People

Ever wonder what separates financially successful people from everyone else? It's often their daily habits. Let's explore some of the routines that set them up for success.

Morning Routines:

How you start your day can set the tone for everything that follows. Many successful people use their mornings to get mentally and physically prepared for the day. This might include reviewing their financial goals, reading a financial news article, or simply setting a budget for the day. Starting your day with a focus on your finances, even if just for a few minutes, keeps your goals top of mind.

Budgeting and Tracking:

One of the most powerful habits you can develop is tracking your spending and sticking to a budget. Successful people know where every dollar goes, and they plan their spending to ensure it aligns with their goals. Whether you use an app, a spreadsheet, or a simple notebook, make it a habit to track your expenses daily. This habit not only helps you stay within your budget but also reveals spending patterns that might need adjustment.

Continuous Learning:

Wealthy individuals often dedicate time each day to learning. This could be reading books on personal finance, following market trends, or listening to podcasts about investing. The financial world is constantly changing, and staying informed is crucial for making smart decisions. Make learning a daily habit, even if it's just for 15 minutes. Over time, this knowledge will compound, just like your investments.

Automating Your Finances

One of the best ways to build wealth is by automating your finances. When you automate, you remove the need for constant decision-making and reduce the chance of human error or temptation.

Automatic Savings:
Set up automatic transfers from your checking account to your savings account. This ensures that you're consistently saving money without even thinking about it.

Whether it's a fixed amount every month or a percentage of your income, automating your savings is a simple yet powerful habit.

Bill Payments:
Late fees can add up quickly and hurt your credit score. By automating your bill payments, you can avoid these unnecessary costs and keep your credit in good shape.

Set up automatic payments for your utilities, credit cards, and any other recurring bills.

Investing Consistently:
Another key to building wealth is to invest consistently, regardless of market conditions. Automating your investments, such as contributions to your retirement account or brokerage account, ensures that you're always putting your money to work. This habit takes the emotion out of investing, helping you to stick to your long-term strategy.

The Habit of Living Below Your Means

Living below your means is the cornerstone of financial success. It's not about depriving yourself but about being mindful of your spending and ensuring that you're saving and investing enough for your future.

Mindful Spending:
Before making any purchase, ask yourself if it's something you really need or if it's just a momentary desire. This habit helps prevent impulse buying, which can quickly drain your finances. By practicing mindful spending, you'll find that you can save more without feeling like you're missing out.

Downsizing:
Look for areas where you can make small cuts without significantly impacting your quality of life. This might mean cooking at home more often, choosing a less expensive phone plan, or driving a more economical car. These small changes can add up to big savings over time.

The Joy of Simplicity:
Embracing a simpler lifestyle can lead to both financial freedom and personal satisfaction. When you focus on what truly matters—health, relationships, experiences—you often find that you need less "stuff" to be happy. This mindset shift can reduce unnecessary spending and help you live a richer life in more ways than one.

The Importance of Patience and Persistence

Building wealth doesn't happen overnight. It requires patience, persistence, and a long-term perspective. Let's explore why these traits are so crucial.

Understanding Compound Interest:
Compound interest is one of the most powerful forces in finance. It's the interest on your interest, and over time, it can turn small, regular investments into a substantial amount of money. The key is to start early and be consistent. The longer your money has to grow, the more powerful the effect of compounding.

Staying the Course:
There will be times when it's tempting to stray from your financial plan—whether it's splurging on a big purchase or pulling out of an investment during a market downturn. Successful people understand the importance of staying the course. They stick to their plan, trusting that their habits will pay off in the long run.

Celebrating Small Wins:
To stay motivated, it's important to recognize and celebrate your progress along the way. Whether it's paying off a credit card, reaching a savings milestone, or making your first investment, take a moment to celebrate. These small wins build momentum and reinforce the positive habits you've developed.

Overcoming Bad Habits

Bad financial habits can be like leaks in a boat—they might seem small, but if left unchecked, they can sink your financial future. Let's look at how to identify and overcome these habits.

Identifying Financial Drains:
Take a close look at your spending and identify any habits that are draining your finances. Common examples include daily coffee runs, frequent dining out, or impulsive online shopping. While these may seem like small expenses, they can add up to significant amounts over time.

Replacing Negative Habits with Positive Ones:
The best way to break a bad habit is to replace it with a good one. If you're prone to impulse buying, try replacing that habit with a savings challenge—every time you resist an impulse purchase, transfer the equivalent amount into your savings. If eating out is your weakness, start meal prepping on Sundays to have healthy, affordable meals ready for the week.

Accountability:
Sometimes, breaking bad habits requires a little extra support. Consider finding a financial accountability partner—someone who shares similar goals and can help you stay on track. You can check in with each other regularly, share successes and challenges, and offer encouragement. Knowing that someone else is invested in your success can be a powerful motivator.

Conclusion: The Long-Term Impact of Wealth-Building Habits

Developing wealth-building habits is like planting seeds—they may not sprout overnight, but with time and care, they will grow into something substantial. By adopting the daily habits of financially successful people, automating your finances, living below your means, and practicing patience and persistence, you're setting yourself up for lifelong financial success.

Remember, it's the small, consistent actions that make the biggest difference. As you continue to build and reinforce these habits, you'll find that wealth creation becomes almost second nature. You're not just changing your financial situation—you're transforming your entire life for the better.

In the next chapter, we'll explore how to protect and grow your wealth through smart investing strategies. With your new habits in place, you'll be ready to take your financial journey to the next level.

6

Smart Investing: Protecting and Growing Your Wealth

Introduction: The Path to Financial Growth

Now that you've laid the foundation with strong financial habits, it's time to focus on growing your wealth through smart investing. Investing isn't just for the wealthy; it's the key to building wealth over time. By putting your money to work, you can achieve financial goals faster and create a more secure future. In this chapter, we'll demystify investing and provide simple strategies to help you start and succeed.

Understanding the Basics of Investing

Investing can seem complicated, but it's simpler than you might think. At its core, investing is about making your money grow by buying assets that increase in value over time. These assets can include stocks, bonds, real estate, or even your own business.

Why Investing Matters:

If you only save money in a bank account, inflation will slowly eat away at its value. Investing allows your money to grow at a rate that outpaces inflation, helping you build real wealth. The earlier you start, the more time your money has to grow, thanks to the power of compound interest.

The Risk-Reward Relationship:

All investments come with some level of risk, but they also offer the potential for reward. Generally, higher-risk investments, like stocks, have the potential for higher returns, while lower-risk investments, like bonds, offer more stability but lower returns. Understanding your risk tolerance—how comfortable you are with the ups and downs of the market—is key to choosing the right investments.

Starting Your Investment Journey

You don't need a lot of money to start investing. The most important step is to begin, even with a small amount.

Set Clear Investment Goals:
Just like with your financial goals, it's important to have clear investment goals. Are you investing for retirement, to buy a home, or to build a college fund for your children? Your goals will help determine your investment strategy.

Types of Investments:
Here are some common types of investments and how they work:

- **Stocks:** When you buy a stock, you're buying a small piece of a company. If the company does well, the value of your stock increases. Stocks can offer high returns, but they also come with higher risk.

- **Bonds**: Bonds are loans you give to companies or governments. In return, they pay you interest over time. Bonds are generally less risky than stocks, making them a good option for those who prefer stability.

- **Mutual Funds and ETFs:** These are collections of stocks or bonds managed by professionals. They allow you to invest in a variety of assets without having to pick individual stocks or bonds yourself. This diversification helps spread risk.

- **Real Estate:** Investing in property can provide both income (through rent) and appreciation (if the property value increases). Real estate can be a good way to diversify your investment portfolio.

Start with What You Know:
If you're new to investing, start with what you're comfortable with. For example, if you understand a particular industry or company, consider investing in it. As you learn more, you can expand into other areas.

The Power of Diversification

Diversification is the practice of spreading your investments across different types of assets to reduce risk. Think of it as not putting all your eggs in one basket.

Why It Matters:
If you invest all your money in one stock and that company fails, you could lose everything. But if you spread your money across different stocks, bonds, and other assets, your risk is reduced. Even if one investment underperforms, others might do well, balancing out your overall portfolio.

How to Diversify:
You can diversify by investing in different types of assets (stocks, bonds, real estate) and within each type (different industries or regions). Mutual funds and ETFs are great tools for diversification because they automatically spread your money across many investments.

Investing for the Long Term

Successful investing is a marathon, not a sprint. The key is to stay patient and focused on your long-term goals.

The Magic of Compounding:
When you reinvest your returns, you start earning returns on your returns. This is called compounding, and over time, it can significantly boost your wealth. The earlier you start investing, the more powerful compounding becomes.

Avoiding Emotional Decisions:
The market will have ups and downs, and it's natural to feel worried during downturns. However, emotional decisions, like selling your investments during a market dip, can hurt your long-term returns. Stick to your plan, and remember that short-term fluctuations are normal.

Regularly Review and Adjust:
While it's important to stay the course, it's also wise to review your investments periodically. As your goals or circumstances change, you may need to adjust your strategy. However, avoid making changes based on short-term market movements—focus on your long-term plan.

Protecting Your Wealth

Growing your wealth is important, but so is protecting it. Here are some ways to safeguard your investments.

Emergency Fund:

Before you invest, make sure you have an emergency fund—enough cash to cover 3-6 months of living expenses. This fund protects you from having to sell investments at a loss if you need money quickly.

Insurance:

Insurance is another tool to protect your wealth. Health, life, and property insurance can prevent financial ruin if something unexpected happens.

Diversification (Again):

Diversification isn't just about growing wealth—it's also about protecting it. A diversified portfolio is less likely to suffer big losses because it's not dependent on the success of a single investment.

Conclusion: Your Path to Financial Freedom

Investing is your ticket to financial freedom. By understanding the basics, starting early, and staying disciplined, you can grow your wealth steadily over time. Remember, it's not about getting rich quickly—it's about making smart, consistent choices that lead to long-term success.

In the next chapter, we'll explore how to manage your investments and finances as they grow, ensuring that you continue to build wealth and move closer to financial independence.

7

Managing and Growing Your Wealth

Introduction: From Building to Managing Wealth

Congratulations! By this stage, you've developed strong financial habits and have begun investing to grow your wealth. But as your wealth increases, so does the responsibility of managing it effectively. In this chapter, we'll explore how to manage your growing wealth to ensure it continues to flourish. We'll cover strategies for monitoring your finances, making adjustments as needed, and protecting what you've built.

Staying on Top of Your Finances

As your wealth grows, it's essential to stay organized and informed. This means regularly monitoring your financial situation to ensure you're on track to meet your goals.

Regular Financial Check-Ins:
Just as you should have regular check-ups for your health, you should also schedule financial check-ins. Set aside time every month to review your budget, track your spending, and evaluate your investments. This helps you stay on top of your finances and make informed decisions.

Using Financial Tools and Apps:
Take advantage of the many financial tools and apps available today. These can help you track your spending, monitor your investments, and even alert you when it's time to re-balance your portfolio. Automating some of these processes can save you time and ensure nothing slips through the cracks.

Keeping an Eye on Your Credit:
Your credit score is a critical component of your financial health. A good credit score can save you money on loans, mortgages, and even insurance. Regularly check your credit report for errors and take steps to improve your score if needed. Simple actions like paying bills on time and reducing credit card balances can make a big difference.

Re-balancing Your Portfolio

As you continue to invest, your portfolio may drift from its original allocation due to the varying performance of your investments. Re-balancing helps you maintain your desired level of risk and ensures that your investment strategy aligns with your goals.

What Is Re-balancing?
Re-balancing involves adjusting your portfolio to return it to its original asset allocation. For example, if you decided on a 70% stocks and 30% bonds allocation, but your stocks have done well and now make up 80% of your portfolio, re-balancing would involve selling some stocks and buying bonds to get back to your original allocation.

When to Re-balance:
You don't need to re-balance constantly. Typically, investors re-balance once or twice a year or when their portfolio drifts significantly from the original allocation (for example, by 5% or more). Some financial tools can automate this process for

you.

Benefits of Re-balancing:

Re-balancing forces you to sell high and buy low, which can enhance your long-term returns. It also helps you stick to your risk tolerance, reducing the chances of taking on more risk than you're comfortable with as your portfolio grows.

Growing Your Wealth Through Diversification

As you manage your wealth, it's crucial to keep diversifying your investments to protect against risk and seize new opportunities.

Exploring New Investment Opportunities:

As your portfolio grows, you might consider adding new types of investments. These could include international stocks, **Real Estate Investment Trusts** (REITs), or even alternative investments like commodities or peer-to-peer lending. Each of these options offers different risk and return profiles, which can further diversify your portfolio.

Dollar-Cost Averaging:

This strategy involves investing a fixed amount of money at regular intervals, regardless of market conditions. By consistently investing, you buy more shares when prices are low and fewer when prices are high, potentially lowering your overall cost. Dollar-cost averaging is an effective way to grow your wealth steadily while reducing the impact of market volatility.

Tax-Efficient Investing:

As your wealth grows, taxes become an increasingly important consideration. Look for ways to minimize your tax burden, such as investing in tax-advantaged accounts like 401(k)s or IRAs, or holding investments for more than a year to benefit from lower long-term capital gains tax rates. Additionally, consider strategies like tax-loss harvesting, where you sell losing investments to offset gains, reducing your overall tax liability.

Protecting Your Wealth

While growing your wealth is essential, protecting it is equally important. This means having a plan in place to safeguard your assets from unexpected events.

Emergency Fund Revisited:

As your wealth increases, it might be wise to reassess your emergency fund. You may want to increase the amount to cover higher living expenses or potential business losses. An adequately funded emergency account ensures that you don't have to dip into your investments when the unexpected happens.

Insurance as a Shield:

Insurance is a critical tool for protecting your wealth. Review your insurance policies regularly to ensure they provide adequate coverage. This includes health insurance, life insurance, homeowners or renters insurance, and, if applicable, disability insurance. For those with significant assets, an umbrella insurance policy can provide extra liability protection beyond the limits of your standard policies.

Estate Planning:
If you haven't already, now is the time to think about estate planning. This involves creating a will, setting up trusts if necessary, and designating beneficiaries for your accounts. Estate planning ensures that your wealth is distributed according to your wishes and can help minimize taxes and legal complications for your heirs.

Seeking Professional Advice

As your financial situation becomes more complex, you might consider working with a financial advisor. A professional can help you navigate investment decisions, tax strategies, and estate planning, ensuring that your wealth continues to grow and is protected for the long term.

When to Hire a Financial Advisor:
If you're feeling overwhelmed by managing your growing wealth or are facing significant life changes like retirement, inheritance, or the sale of a business, a financial advisor can provide valuable guidance. Look for an advisor who is a fiduciary, meaning they are legally required to act in your best interest.

Choosing the Right Advisor:

Not all financial advisors are the same. Some specialize in investment management, while others offer comprehensive financial planning services. Take the time to interview potential advisors, asking about their experience, fees, and investment philosophy to ensure they align with your goals.

Conclusion: The Journey Continues

Managing and growing your wealth is an ongoing process. As you continue on your financial journey, stay proactive, regularly review your goals and strategies, and be willing to adapt as your circumstances change. By doing so, you'll not only preserve the wealth you've worked so hard to build but also continue to grow it, bringing you closer to financial independence and the life you envision.

In the next chapter, we'll explore how to achieve financial independence and retire early, giving you the freedom to live life on your terms.

8

Financial Independence: Achieving Freedom and Early Retirement

Introduction: What Is Financial Independence?

Financial independence means having enough wealth to cover your living expenses without relying on a traditional job. It's about achieving the freedom to choose how you spend your time, whether that's pursuing passions, traveling the world, or simply enjoying a more relaxed lifestyle. For many, financial independence also means the possibility of retiring early, often referred to as "FIRE" (**Financial Independence, Retire Early**).

In this chapter, we'll explore how to achieve financial independence, the strategies that can help you retire early, and how to maintain your financial freedom once you've reached it.

Defining Your Financial Independence Number

Your financial independence number is the amount of money you need to achieve financial freedom. This number varies depending on your lifestyle, location, and personal goals.

Calculating Your Number:
To calculate your financial independence number, start by estimating your annual living expenses. A common rule of thumb is to multiply that amount by 25 to 30. This is based on the 4% rule, which suggests that you can withdraw 4% of your investments each year in retirement without running out of money. For example, if you need $40,000 per year to live comfortably, your financial independence number would be $1,000,000 ($40,000 x 25).

Adjusting for Lifestyle:
Your financial independence number should reflect the lifestyle you want in retirement. If you plan to travel extensively, move to a higher-cost area, or take up expensive hobbies, you may need to save more. Conversely, if you plan to downsize or move to a more affordable location, you may require less.

Strategies to Achieve Financial Independence

Reaching financial independence requires a combination of saving, investing, and lifestyle choices. Here are some key strategies to help you get there.

Aggressive Saving:
The more you save, the faster you can reach financial independence. Aim to save at least 50% of your income, if possible. This may require significant lifestyle adjustments, such as cutting unnecessary expenses, downsizing your home, or living in a lower-cost area. The more you save, the more you can invest, accelerating your path to financial freedom.

Maximizing Income:
Increasing your income can significantly speed up your journey to financial independence. This could involve negotiating a higher salary, taking on a side hustle, or starting a business. The key is to channel any extra income directly into your savings and investments rather than increasing your spending.

Smart Investing:
Investing is crucial to growing your wealth and achieving financial independence. Focus on building a diversified portfolio that aligns with your risk tolerance and goals. Consider low-cost index funds, real estate, and other growth-oriented investments. The earlier you start investing, the more you can benefit from compound growth.

Avoiding Lifestyle Inflation:
Lifestyle inflation occurs when your spending increases as

your income rises. While it's tempting to upgrade your lifestyle with every raise or bonus, resisting this urge is key to achieving financial independence. Instead, keep your expenses steady and direct any additional income towards your savings and investments.

Planning for Early Retirement

If early retirement is part of your financial independence plan, there are additional factors to consider. Retiring early means your savings need to last longer, and you may face unique challenges, such as accessing retirement accounts before the standard age.

Building a Larger Nest Egg:
　Since retiring early means you'll need to support yourself for more years, you may need a larger nest egg than someone retiring at a traditional age. This might mean saving more aggressively or working a few extra years to ensure you have enough to last.

Healthcare Considerations:
　Healthcare is a significant expense, especially if you retire before qualifying for government programs like Medicare. Be sure to factor in the cost of health insurance and medical expenses when calculating your financial independence number. Researching affordable healthcare options, such as **Health Savings Accounts** (HSAs) or marketplace insurance plans, can help manage these costs.

Accessing Retirement Funds Early:

If you retire before 59½, you may face penalties for withdrawing money from certain retirement accounts like 401(k)s or IRAs. However, there are ways to access these funds penalty-free, such as setting up a Roth IRA conversion ladder or using **Substantially Equal Periodic Payments** (SEPPs). These strategies can be complex, so consider consulting a financial advisor to ensure you're making the right moves.

Maintaining Financial Independence

Achieving financial independence is a significant milestone, but maintaining it requires ongoing vigilance and smart financial management.

Creating a Withdrawal Strategy:

Once you've achieved financial independence, you'll need a strategy for withdrawing money from your investments. The 4% rule is a popular guideline, but it's important to remain flexible. In years when the market performs well, you might withdraw a bit more, while in leaner years, you may need to tighten your belt. The goal is to ensure your money lasts for the duration of your retirement.

Continued Investment:

Even in retirement, it's wise to keep a portion of your portfolio invested in growth assets like stocks. This helps combat inflation and ensures your money continues to grow over time. A common approach is to maintain a diversified portfolio with a mix of stocks, bonds, and other assets that reflect your risk tolerance and income needs.

Monitoring Expenses:

Just because you're financially independent doesn't mean you can stop paying attention to your spending. Regularly review your expenses to ensure they align with your budget and long-term goals. Avoiding unnecessary splurges and staying within your means will help you maintain your financial freedom.

Considering Part-Time Work or Hobbies:

Some people choose to continue working part-time or turn hobbies into income streams even after achieving financial independence. This can provide additional income, reduce the need to draw down on your investments, and keep you engaged and fulfilled.

Conclusion: Living the Life You Want

Financial independence isn't just about having enough money; it's about having the freedom to live life on your terms. Whether that means retiring early, pursuing passions, or simply having more time to spend with loved ones, financial independence offers a world of possibilities.

As you work towards and eventually achieve financial independence, remember that the journey is just as important as the destination. Stay disciplined, be patient, and enjoy the freedom that comes with knowing you're in control of your financial future.

In the final chapter, we'll discuss how to leave a legacy, ensuring that the wealth and wisdom you've accumulated can benefit future generations.

9

leaving a Legacy: Ensuring Your Wealth and Wisdom Live On

Introduction: The Meaning of Legacy

Achieving financial independence and growing your wealth are remarkable accomplishments. However, the true impact of your financial journey is often measured by the legacy you leave behind. A legacy is not just about money; it's about the values, lessons, and contributions that endure long after you're gone. In this chapter, we'll explore how to create a lasting legacy that reflects your life's work and positively influences future generations.

Defining Your Legacy

Leaving a legacy starts with defining what you want that legacy to be. This involves reflecting on your values, priorities, and the impact you wish to have on the world.

Personal Values and Vision:
What are the principles that have guided you throughout your life? What causes or issues are you passionate about? Your legacy should reflect the values that are most important to you. Whether it's supporting education, contributing to scientific research, or ensuring your family's financial security, your legacy should align with your deepest convictions.

Financial vs. Non-Financial Legacy:
While many people focus on the financial aspects of their legacy, such as passing on wealth to heirs, non-financial legacies can be equally im pactful. This could include sharing your life experiences, documenting family history, mentoring others, or contributing to causes that matter to you. Think about the ways in which you can leave a mark beyond just money.

Estate Planning: Protecting Your Financial Legacy

To ensure that your financial legacy is preserved and distributed according to your wishes, it's essential to have a comprehensive estate plan in place.

Creating a Will:
A will is a legal document that outlines how you want your assets to be distributed after your death. Without a will, state laws will determine how your estate is divided, which may not

align with your wishes. In your will, you can specify who will inherit your assets, name guardians for minor children, and designate an executor to carry out your instructions.

Setting Up Trusts:

Trusts are legal entities that hold and manage assets on behalf of your beneficiaries. They can be a powerful tool for controlling how and when your wealth is distributed. For example, a trust can provide for the education of your grandchildren, support a family member with special needs, or donate to charity over time. Trusts can also offer tax benefits and protect your assets from creditors or legal disputes.

Minimizing Taxes:

Estate taxes can significantly reduce the amount of wealth you pass on to your heirs. Fortunately, there are strategies to minimize these taxes, such as gifting assets during your lifetime, establishing charitable trusts, or setting up an irrevocable life insurance trust. Working with a tax advisor or estate planner can help you identify the best options for your situation.

Designating Beneficiaries:

For retirement accounts, life insurance policies, and other financial accounts, be sure to designate beneficiaries. These designations supersede your will, so it's crucial to keep them updated, especially after major life events like marriage, divorce, or the birth of a child.

Passing on Values and Wisdom

While passing on wealth is important, sharing your values and life lessons can have an even more profound impact on your family and community.

Writing an Ethical Will:
An ethical will is a document that shares your values, life lessons, hopes, and dreams with your loved ones. Unlike a legal will, it's not about distributing assets, but about passing on your wisdom and beliefs. This could include stories about your life, advice for future generations, or your thoughts on important issues. An ethical will can be a powerful way to ensure that your values live on.

Teaching Financial Literacy:
One of the greatest gifts you can give your heirs is the knowledge of how to manage money wisely. Consider holding family meetings to discuss financial topics, offering to pay for financial education, or mentoring younger family members as they start their financial journeys. By equipping them with the skills they need to manage their inheritance, you help ensure that your wealth will be preserved and used wisely.

Documenting Family History:
Sharing your family's history and traditions can create a sense of continuity and identity for future generations. This could involve writing a memoir, recording video messages, or creating a family tree. By preserving your family's story, you help future generations understand where they came from and the values that have shaped their lives.

Charitable Giving: Leaving a Legacy of Generosity

Charitable giving is a powerful way to leave a legacy that extends beyond your family. By supporting causes you care about, you can make a lasting difference in the world.

Choosing Causes You Care About:
Reflect on the causes that matter most to you, whether it's education, healthcare, environmental conservation, or social justice. Your charitable legacy should reflect your passions and the impact you want to have on society.

Creating a Donor-Advised Fund:
A **Donor-Advised Fund (DAF)** is a charitable giving account that allows you to make a donation, receive an immediate tax benefit, and recommend grants to charities over time. **DAFs** are a flexible and efficient way to manage your charitable giving, and they can be a great way to involve your family in philanthropy.

Establishing a Foundation:
For those with significant wealth, establishing a private foundation can be a powerful way to leave a charitable legacy. A foundation allows you to make grants to charities, fund scholarships, and support causes that align with your values. It also provides a structure for involving your family in philanthropy and ensuring that your charitable work continues after your death.

Legacy Gifts:
Legacy gifts, also known as planned gifts, are donations that

you arrange to make at a future date, usually through your estate. This could include leaving a portion of your estate to a charity in your will, designating a charity as a beneficiary of your retirement account, or donating a life insurance policy. Legacy gifts ensure that your philanthropy continues even after you're gone.

Involving Your Family in Legacy Planning

Creating a lasting legacy is often a family affair. Involving your loved ones in the process can help ensure that your legacy reflects your collective values and that your heirs are prepared to carry it forward.

Family Meetings:
Regular family meetings can be a great way to discuss your legacy plans and ensure everyone is on the same page. These meetings provide an opportunity to share your values, discuss your estate plan, and answer any questions your heirs may have. They also help build a sense of unity and shared purpose.

Encouraging Family Philanthropy:
Involving your family in charitable giving can be a meaningful way to pass on your values. Consider creating a family charitable fund or involving your children and grandchildren in the decision-making process for your charitable donations. This not only teaches the importance of giving back but also strengthens family bonds.

Preparing the Next Generation:

Ensure that your heirs are prepared to manage the wealth they will inherit. This might involve providing financial education, introducing them to your financial advisors, or setting up trusts that distribute assets over time rather than in a lump sum. Preparing the next generation helps ensure that your legacy is preserved and that your wealth is used in ways that align with your values.

Conclusion: The Enduring Impact of a Thoughtful Legacy

Leaving a legacy is about more than just money—it's about the lasting impact you have on the people you love and the world around you. By carefully planning your legacy, you can ensure that your wealth and wisdom are preserved, your values are upheld, and your contributions continue to make a difference long after you're gone.

As you move forward, remember that building and leaving a legacy is a dynamic process. It's never too early or too late to start thinking about the mark you want to leave on the world. By taking intentional steps now, you can create a legacy that truly reflects who you are and what you stand for, providing inspiration and guidance for generations to come.

10

Celebrating Your Journey and Paying It Forward

"BEYOND THE DOLLAR: TRANSFORMING YOUR MINDSET FOR LIFELONG FINANCIAL SUCCESS"

Introduction: A Time to Reflect and Rejoice

As we arrive at the final chapter of "Beyond the Dollar," it's time to take a moment to celebrate your journey. You've explored the depths of financial empowerment, transformed your mindset, and laid the foundation for a life of purpose and fulfillment. Now, it's important to reflect on how far you've come, recognize your achievements, and consider how you can pay it forward to help others on their journey. This chapter will guide you through the process of celebrating your successes, expressing gratitude, and making a lasting impact by giving back.

Celebrating Milestones: Recognizing Your Achievements

One of the most powerful things you can do at the end of a journey is to celebrate your milestones. Acknowledging your progress not only boosts your confidence but also motivates you to continue striving for more.

Taking Stock of Your Successes:
Reflect on the goals you've achieved throughout your financial and personal growth journey. Whether it was overcoming debt, building a robust investment portfolio, starting a passion project, or finding balance in your life, each success is worth celebrating. Take time to list these accomplishments and savor the satisfaction that comes from knowing you've made significant strides.

Rewarding Yourself:
Celebration can take many forms, from treating yourself to a special experience to simply taking a moment of quiet reflection. Consider rewarding yourself in a way that aligns with your values and brings you joy. Whether it's a small indulgence or a meaningful gesture, make sure to mark your achievements in a way that feels fulfilling to you.

Sharing Your Success:

Celebrations are even sweeter when shared with others. Consider sharing your journey and successes with friends, family, or a community of like-minded individuals. Not only does this reinforce your achievements, but it also inspires others to pursue their own goals. Your story can be a beacon of hope and motivation for those who are just starting their journey.

The Power of Gratitude: Appreciating the Journey

Gratitude is a powerful tool that can enhance your sense of well-being and keep you grounded. By expressing gratitude for your journey, you acknowledge the support, opportunities, and experiences that have shaped your success.

Reflecting on the Lessons Learned:

Every step of your journey has been a learning experience. Reflect on the lessons you've learned, both from successes and setbacks. How have these lessons shaped who you are today? What insights have you gained about yourself, your values, and your approach to life? By recognizing these lessons, you appreciate the growth that has come from your journey.

Expressing Gratitude to Those Who Helped:

No journey is made alone. Think about the people who have supported you along the way—mentors, family, friends, colleagues, and even those who challenged you to grow. Take time to express your gratitude to these individuals. A simple note, a heartfelt conversation, or a small gesture of thanks can go a long way in acknowledging the impact they've had on your life.

Gratitude for the Challenges:
Challenges are often our greatest teachers. Consider the obstacles you've faced and how they've contributed to your growth. Expressing gratitude for these challenges may seem counter intuitive, but it allows you to see the silver lining in difficult experiences and appreciate the resilience and strength you've developed as a result.

Paying It Forward: Making a Lasting Impact

As you reflect on your journey, consider how you can pay it forward and help others achieve their own version of success. Giving back not only enriches the lives of others but also deepens your own sense of purpose.

Mentoring the Next Generation:
One of the most impactful ways to pay it forward is by mentoring others. Whether you mentor young professionals, aspiring entrepreneurs, or individuals in your community, sharing your knowledge and experience can help them navigate their own journeys. Your guidance can provide the support and encouragement they need to overcome challenges and achieve their goals.

Supporting Causes That Matter:
Consider how you can use your financial success to support

causes that align with your values. This could involve charitable donations, volunteering your time, or advocating for issues that are important to you. By contributing to the greater good, you create a ripple effect that extends far beyond your immediate circle, making a positive impact on the world.

Creating Opportunities for Others:

If you have the means, think about how you can create opportunities for others to succeed. This might involve starting a scholarship fund, investing in social enterprises, or providing resources for those who lack access to education or financial tools. By empowering others, you help build a more equitable and prosperous future for all.

Continuing the Journey: A Lifelong Commitment

Even as you celebrate your achievements and give back to others, remember that the journey is ongoing. Personal and financial growth is a lifelong commitment, and there are always new horizons to explore.

Setting New Aspirations:

With your current goals achieved, consider what's next on your horizon. What new challenges do you want to tackle? What passions do you want to pursue? By setting new aspirations, you keep the momentum going and ensure that your life remains dynamic and fulfilling.

Staying Connected to Your Purpose:

As you continue on your journey, stay connected to your core purpose. Your purpose will evolve as you grow, but its essence will remain a guiding light in your life. Regularly revisit your values, passions, and goals to ensure that your actions align with your evolving sense of purpose.

Living a Legacy Every Day:
Your legacy is not just what you leave behind, but how you live each day. By embodying the principles and values you've cultivated throughout this journey, you create a living legacy that inspires others. Live with intention, kindness, and a commitment to making a positive impact, and your legacy will naturally unfold.

This chapter concludes the book, "Beyond the Dollar." As you step into the next chapter of your life, remember that the principles and insights you've gained here are just the beginning. The future is yours to shape, and the possibilities are limitless.

11

Conclusion

Conclusion: The Ongoing Adventure

"Beyond the Dollar" has been a journey of transformation, growth, and empowerment. You've learned how to manage your finances, cultivate a success-oriented mindset, and live a life of purpose and meaning. But more than that, you've embarked on an adventure that continues beyond these pages.

As you move forward, carry with you the knowledge that you have the power to shape your life in profound ways. Celebrate your achievements, express gratitude for the journey, and pay it forward by helping others on their paths. The adventure never truly ends—it evolves, expands, and deepens with each new experience.

Thank you for joining this journey. May you continue to grow, thrive, and live a life that goes beyond the dollar, filled with purpose, passion, and lasting fulfillment.

CONCLUSION

* * *

Resources:

Covey SR. The seven habits of highly effective people. Natl Med Leg J. 1991;2(2):8. PMID: 1747433.

Dominguez, J., & Robin, V. (1992a). *Your money or your life*. http://newroadmap.pbworks.com/f/StudyGuide-ver-BSG4-ORIGINAL.pdf

Fine, B., & Milonakis D. (2010). From economics imperialism to Freakonomics, the shifting boundaries between economics and other social sciences. *Choice Reviews Online, 47*(05), 47–2682. https://doi.org/10.5860/choice.47-2682

Locke, E. A. (2013). New developments in goal setting and task performance. In *Routledge E Books*. https://doi.org/10.4324/9780203082744

(2023b). Morgan Housel: The psychology of money: timeless lessons on wealth, greed, and happiness (Harriman House, 2020). *Financial Markets and Portfolio Management*. https://doi.org/10.1007/s11408-022-00424-9

Kiyosaki, R. T. (2009). *Rich dad, poor dad: What the rich teach their kids about Money—That the poor and the middle class do not!*

http://ci.nii.ac.jp/ncid/BA50082780

Locke, E. A., & Latham, G. P. (2006). New directions in Goal-Setting Theory. *Current Directions in Psychological Science, 15*(5), 265–268. https://doi.org/10.1111/j.1467-8721.2006.00449.x

Tosi, H. L. (1991). A Theory of Goal Setting and Task Performance A Theory of Goal Setting and Task Performance, by Locke Edwin A. and Latham Gary P.. Englewood Cliffs, NJ: Prentice-Hall, 1990. *Academy of Management Review, 16*(2), 480–483. https://doi.org/10.5465/amr.1991.4278976

Long, A. A. (2009). Reading Seneca: Stoic Philosophy at Rome. *The Philosophical Review, 118*(3), 378–381. https://doi.org/10.1215/00318108-2009-005

Tolle, E. (1997). *The Power of Now: A Guide to Spiritual Enlightenment.* http://ci.nii.ac.jp/ncid/BA56671795

Shefrin, H. (2003). Beyond Greed and Fear: Understanding behavioral finance and the psychology of investing. *Choice Reviews Online, 41*(03), 41–1676. https://doi.org/10.5860/choice.41-1676

Stanley, T. J. (2004). The millionaire next door. *An Exploration of the Habits and Mindset That Differentiates Wealthy Individuals From the Rest of Society.* http://www.marshallcf.com/assets/book_reviews/Millionaire%20Next%20Door-w.pdf

Hill, N. (1937a). *Think & grow rich.* https://en.wikipedia.org/wiki/Think_and_Grow_Rich

About the Author

A wife and mother of three teenage boys, [Rowdean Kurasch-Macharzina] has been married for 20 years and is originally from Jamaica, now living in Germany. Her journey from the vibrant Caribbean to the heart of Europe has shaped her perspective on life, wealth, and family. With a deep love for traveling, she enjoys exploring new cultures, which has opened her mind to different ways of thinking about success.

In between her adventures, she finds joy in the simple things—like cooking delicious meals for her family, curling up with a good book, or enjoying quiet moments with her partner. Reading widely and watching her favorite shows during television time are her favorite ways to unwind.

Her passion for understanding life beyond material wealth and her desire to inspire others to achieve lifelong financial success led her to write *Beyond the Dollar*. With practical insights and a focus on mindset, she empowers readers to not only transform their finances but also their outlook on what true success really means.

www.ingramcontent.com/pod-product-compliance
Lightning Source LLC
Chambersburg PA
CBHW070356230526
45471CB00006B/2594